IT'S TIME FOR THE BIG QUESTION

How to get him to propose the way you want it. Original wedding proposal ideas with detailed guidelines.

By S. L. Giger

"Being deeply loved by someone gives you strength, while loving someone deeply gives you courage."
– Lao Tzu.

Free Download

Heart of Power – Awakening of the Siren

Despite being a mystical beauty with supernatural powers beyond any human abilities, there is this one guy who manages to completely get under her skin.

17-year-old Serena can't escape her true destiny any longer. She is transformed into a Siren and has to get used to a new name, new powers and constantly attracting every man's glance. Guided by her new family members, she faces the challenge of attending High School among humans without appearing different. When Alex, the most attractive guy, reciprocates her love, she seems to finally accept her fate.

However, two secrets are yet to be revealed, and Serena has to make a tough choice.

This is the compelling first novel in the Heart of Power trilogy. S. L. Giger manages to add a refreshing breeze to fantasy by successfully introducing us to the world of Sirens in our modern age.

To receive the book write me an e-mail with the subject: A Sketch of What You Mean to Me. Write the 1. phrase of this first chapter in the body of the mail.
swissmissstories@gmail.com

Contents

It's time for the big question 3

A romantic wedding proposal 9

  1. Candlelight picknick in nature 9

    The beach 10

    The raft 13

  2. The fancy meal 17

  3. Say it with flowers.............................19

  4. A sky full of fireworks........................21

A proposal that involves a hobby 23

  1. Dance Flash Mob................................23

  2. Well orchestrated 26

  3. Hidden T-Shirts..................................27

  4. Movie Credits 29

  5. Let the pet be the messenger 31

  6. Become part of a play 33

3 Unexpected surprises 37

  1. Steal the show at a concert 37

  2. Bake it into a cake.............................39

  3. Melt it into ice cream........................41

  4. Hide it in the popcorn 43

  5. Let her solve the riddle 44

  6. Surprise via the speakers (train or plane)..........46

Personal Notes..48

Afterthoughts 49

Dear ladies and gentlemen

Congratulations! You have thought about it thoroughly and you came to the decision that you want to get married. Probably, in our modern day and age, the gentleman hasn't asked permission of the parents of the lady and the lady isn't completely in the dark about the feelings of the gentleman because the couple would have spoken about their feelings for each other and their life plans beforehand. So, the guy now might think: Why on earth, if my girlfriend is allowed to make decisions on her own, work, and perhaps even earns a bigger salary than me, should I have to be the one to pop the questions of all questions? Can't we just decide to get married and get it over with? Or why doesn't she just ask me herself?

Of course, those thoughts are justified, and it would be socially accepted if the lady asks the gentleman. However, even with the burning topic of emancipation, it's just good to stick to some traditions. Not to lose touch to a tradition that will give a lady a splendid memory which she'll love to talk about her whole life afterward. A tradition which gives the gentleman to be the knight in shining armor or the superhero he surely wants to be for his lady.
That the longing for this tradition of the gentleman proposing to the lady is still very present. Or why would there otherwise be such a big demand for this book?

So, dear gentleman, even if you'd rather not do the whole circus about one small question, do it for the love of your life. Because, I sure hope the lady you want to marry is the love of your life and then if you could do something quite simple which would make your lady tremendously happy and give her a long-lasting memory of bliss, wouldn't you want to do it for her?

Up to now, your lady might seem like a very independent woman to you and you don't see the point in the tradition of asking to marry her. However, in case you do want to have children, it will be a huge change for the lady. Once she is a mom, there is no going back. She will never be first anymore. She will always put your child's needs ahead of her own. That's just what happens to women. No matter how much emancipation we have gone through, it's still our true instinct to take care of our family. And as you know, being married and having a family won't always be a shiny walk in the park. There will be hardships to go through, but you will manage because you love each other and committed to each other. So, think ahead and use your wedding proposal as a way to say thank you. Thank you for the good times you had and for the wonderful times that are yet to come. Give your lady a proposal which will bring a smile to her face at any moment of her life from then on.
And, dear gentleman, no matter in what way you ask the question, get down on your knee. It's just a part

that belongs to the tradition and is like a signal function that the lady realizes that what is happening is really happening.

Now that you know why the gentleman still needs to propose to the lady, as follows you find detailed guidelines to plan the perfect wedding proposal for your relationship.

So, it's time to find the perfect wedding proposal for your lady. With every proposal you read, bear in mind that the proposal needs to be about her. So, think first about what she'd enjoy and second, what you would like as well. Remember, if you could make a dream come true for her, it will be the best reward for yourself as well.
It goes without saying that in case you need people to help you with your proposal, they have to be absolutely trustworthy so that nothing can go wrong, and your lady doesn't find out about it previously.
Last but not least, during your proposal, always say something about what you appreciate about your lady and that you don't want to spend your life with anybody else but her. Then, you ask her to marry you.

Personal Notes

A ROMANTIC WEDDING PROPOSAL

Perhaps those aren't the most original wedding proposals as they have been used in movies or in the real life many times. And you know why they are used often? Because they are big classics. Most women fall for romantic gestures and therefore, she will be very happy when she will receive a romantic wedding proposal. Moreover, even though romantic proposals are so well suited for this occasion, they aren't done enough. Today, many couples simply decide to get married and that's it. Where is the magic that love usually brings with it?

1. Candlelight picknick in nature

She likes the outdoors and if she sees candles, her romantic heart is touched, and her eyes will sparkle like the flames themselves, as if it were a competition? Then, this kind of wedding proposal will be perfect for her.
First, you need to decide where in the outdoors you want to pop the question. Does she like the beach? Then, find a quiet spot at a beach or a lake. If she likes hiking, lead her on top of a local hill (since you can only spot candles in the dark, it can't be a difficult hike because that might get too dangerous. Or, at least bring two head torches for the return hike). Do you know a great place in the forest? Near a lovely

waterfall? Find a place that means a lot to her or even a place that means something to both of you.

Read on to find two of the outdoor suggestions explained in detail. Simply adapt the planning of these suggestions for the picknick in the place of your choice.

The beach

Planning:

- Pick the perfect, quiet, and beautiful spot at a beach.
- Pick a night with a good weather forecast (little wind)
- Get a friend or two who will spend the afternoon with your lady.
- Buy the candles (50-100 depending on how big of an area you want to cover) and the things you need for the picknick: blanket, cups, plates, silverware, napkins and the food and drinks of your choice (for example a salad, sandwiches, some olives or other antipasti, and wine)
- Bring a torch for the way back

How the proposal should play out

Your friends have to make sure that your lady has a good
time in the afternoon.
While she is busy, you have time to set up the candles
along the path to your beach spot and around the blanket.
At dawn (15min before the agreed time with your friends),
you can light the candles, starting at the beginning of the
path, leading to the blanket. Set out the olives and some
wine.

Your friends will bring your lady to the beginning of the
path which leads down to your secret beach spot at the
time you told them. They should all be surprised to see the
candles and then tell your lady to follow the path on her
own, as your friends need to get something in the car or
make up some other excuse why they can't go with her
now.
You will be waiting for her standing on the blanket. You
want to make sure that she knows it's you right away since
she probably didn't expect you here and won't know what
is going on.

You lead her onto the blanket and tell her that you wanted
to do something nice for her and therefore planned an
outdoor candlelight dinner for her.
Then, you open the food basket and you enjoy the dinner
with her. When dinner comes to an end, you tell her that
you have another surprise for her. You take out the case
with the ring and get onto your knee. Then, you say the
nice words you prepared and ask her to marry you.

After she said yes

Now, you have several options.

1. If you want to go celebrate with the same friends who already spent the afternoon with your lady and perhaps some other friends as well, you order them back one hour after they dropped her off. They can collect the candles along the path so that you won't leave behind any rubbish. They will also help you clean the spot around the blanket and help you carry the things back into the car. Afterward, you can head to a bar and celebrate your future.

2. Since you are in a secluded and nice spot you might want to keep it secluded and enjoy a romantic evening together with your lady. Then, just keep in mind to clean up all the candles once the two of you leave. It's easy to spot the now possibly dead candles in the light of your torch.

3. If you want to enjoy the night with only your lady but don't want to interrupt the fun with cleaning up on your way back, you order your friends to come and clean up two hours or so after they dropped off your lady and they will clean up for you while you can have a nice evening with her wherever you want.

The raft

Preparation:

- Chose a raft on a lake that isn't very busy
- Pick a night with a good weather forecast
- Set a date with your lady
- Buy the candles (50-100 depending on how big an area you want to cover) and the things you need for the picknick: blanket, cups, plates, silverware, napkins and the food and drinks of your choice (for example a salad, sandwiches, some olives or other antipasti, and wine). Plus, pack some towels in the basket as it might get cold during the picknick since you are wet. You also need a floating device to transport the things to the raft.
- Get a friend or two who will decorate the raft for you
- Bring a torch for the way back

How the proposal should play out

Previously to the special day, you might have to inform a lifeguard or anyone who is in charge of the lake with the raft about your special plan. I'm sure they'll let you do it if the lake isn't busy and you'll clean up after yourself.

You then spend the afternoon together with your lady away from the lake or you pick her up shortly before dawn and then drive to the lake with her.

Your friends have set up the candles on the raft and lit them in the meantime. They also placed the floating device with the basket with the picknick on the raft and marked it with a well visible sheet of paper which says: One-time surprise for my girlfriend. Please, let us have the raft tonight and don't touch anything. Thank you very much for your understanding, YOUR NAME.

Your arrival needs to be well timed with your friends who set up the candles so that they don't burn down before you arrive. However, they need enough time to get to shore and disappear without being noticed by your lady. Perhaps, they can even stay close by and keep an eye on the raft so that no other people spoil the surprise.

Once you arrive at the lake, you point out the candles on the raft to her and suggest that you go check it out. Of course, you have to let your lady know beforehand that it's your intention to have an evening swim together. The two of you swim out to the raft and you climb onto it. Then, you can say; "Tadaa, I planned a little picknick for you."
At first, she probably won't believe how you could have planned this, but there it says your name on the basket with the food.

So, you enjoy your picknick and when it gets to the end, you tell your lady that you have something to ask her. You get onto your knee and tell her how you feel about her. Then, you ask her to marry you. (I'm not sure whether you should store an expensive ring on the raft while you aren't there, so either, propose without a ring or if the ring is important to her, propose with a cheap, costume jewelry ring, and tell her that she gets the real one later. You Can find beautiful accessory rings starting at $3. Before she touches it, she won't even realize it's not real silver or gold.)

Once you want to swim back to shore, don't forget to collect all the candles and safely transport them back to shore in the floating device with the basket and everything else.

It's your choice whether you want to meet your friends now to go celebrate together or whether you let them know in the beginning that the evening will belong to you and your lady afterward.

Personal Notes

2. The fancy meal

Your lady likes dressing up, putting on nice makeup, and going out to a fancy restaurant once in a while? Then, she is making it easy for you as you can go along with this classic but impactful proposal.

Planning:

- Reserve the fancy restaurant and inform the restaurant about your intention.
- Let the waiter be on standby and have him come out with either champagne or a cake with sparklers after she said yes. (It depends on whether she is more of a toasting kind of woman or the "you can eat cake for any kind of occasion" kind of woman).
- Set a date with your lady.

How the proposal should play out

You bring your lady to the restaurant and are the perfect gentlemen (which of course, you usually are) throughout the dinner.
After the main course, you take your lady's hands across the table and start telling her how you feel about her. Then, you get up and get down onto your knee and ask her to marry you.

She will say yes, and in case it's not a private booth in a Japanese restaurant, the other guests might clap. At that moment, the waiter will also come out with the cake or champagne to congratulate you.
Then, you enjoy your dessert and both of you can be even happier now, about what a nice dinner this is.

PERSONAL NOTES

____

____

____

____

____

____

____

____

____

____

____

____

____

____

____

____

3. Say it with flowers

Your lady likes flowers or spring and summer or when everything is lush? Then, this proposal might be the right one for you.

Planning:

- Buy or pick as many flowers as you need to decorate the whole bedroom (or living room)
- You need vases or high glasses to place the flowers in
- Also, buy some extra flowers or rose petals to strew on the floor and show her the way to the decorated room
- Find the perfect timing. She needs to be out of the house, but you have to know at about what time she will return
- Cool the champagne or anything else you want to celebrate with in the fridge once the lady is out of the house (before that, you have to hide it somewhere)

How the proposal should play out

On the day that you picked, you bring the flowers to the house when you are sure that your lady isn't there. You decorate the room of your choice with placing vases with flowers in as many places as you can. Then, you also make a path of rose petals from the door to the decorated room.

In the center of the decorated room, you could form a big heart out of flowers on the ground. In this heart, you could be waiting with flowers in your hand. When your lady arrives, you smile at her and start telling her how you feel about her. Then, you pop the big question.

If you don't want to talk so much, you could also use flower petals and write: WILL YOU MARRY ME in the middle of the room or on your bed. You can hide in the corner of a room and show yourself once she has understood the question. Then, also you should tell her why you want to marry her, and perhaps ask her orally, in case she hasn't answered to your written message because she was so surprised.

PERSONAL NOTES

____

____

____

____

____

____

____

____

____

4. A sky full of fireworks

The eyes of your lady sparkle as if it was her birthday and Christmas combined when she sees fireworks in the sky? If there is a festival with fireworks near you, she pulls you to the best place to see the show in the sky? Then, perhaps you should give her one more opportunity to enjoy fireworks. This proposal is the only one where the lady might not believe that you actually planned those fireworks. So, have your friends take some pictures of how they light them. Later, they can show the pictures to the happily engaged couple.

Preparation:

- Organize the fireworks
- Find a good location to send them to the sky (make sure you are allowed to light fireworks in that area)
- Find a good spot to watch the fireworks from
- Get some friends who will set up the fireworks and then light them for you when you are ready
- Have something ready with which you can celebrate. Either, hide a bottle of champagne with two glasses in the car. If you are somewhere far away from cars, you could also already visit this spot earlier and hide the bottle and the cups behind a tree or a bush

and hope that it's still there. That will make it even more believable for your lady that you actually planned the fireworks and this whole proposal and that it wasn't just a spontaneous idea after you saw someone else's fireworks.

How the proposal should play out

Perhaps, you want to take your lady out for a nice dinner before the fireworks. Then, you take her on a walk or drive to the spot to view the fireworks. You tell her that you have a surprise for her. You reveal that in some minutes, there will be fireworks over there (you point to the spot where they will be) and that they are just for her.

When the fireworks are over, you can tell her, that you want to give her the sky or more. That you want to do anything to make her happy because when she is happy, you are happy. Then, you get down on your knee and ask her to marry you.

After she said yes

Now, you are both on a high and this needs to be celebrated with something. Bring out the drink from its hiding spot and cheers to your joint future.

A PROPOSAL THAT INVOLVES A HOBBY

While almost every woman loves a romantic wedding proposal you can make it even more personal if you involve a hobby of hers. After all, she spends a lot of time of her life doing that hobby. Even if you want to be the number one leisure activity, she loves most, you can still show that you support her to evolve her personality. What better way to do that than organizing a secret wedding proposal together with people or utensils from her hobby?

1. Dance Flash Mob

Is she in any kind of dance group or club or do you even dance a partner dance together? Great, this will be a proposal the people around you will enjoy as well!

Preparation

- Get the dance group to plan a flash mob without her getting wind of it (it doesn't need to be anything fancy, it can even be the same choreography that she knows).
- Set a date and time with them where they need to show up.
- Either plan a date with your lady around that location or get some friends of hers to bring

her to the location so that first she will be surprised about the flash mob and then she will be even more surprised when you are there, too.

How the proposal should play out

For example, you picked the market square in your town as the location. Let's go with scenario one where you are there with your lady. Perhaps, you are strolling across the square "by coincidence" or maybe you are sitting in an outdoor café. Out of the blue, a loud boombox announces the start of a song. Then, the flash mob starts, with dancers showing up around you. Of course, the dancers were in disguise or hiding before so that the lady didn't notice they were there before the song started.
In case it's a partner dance choreography, you can get her to dance with you in the middle of the song.

If you weren't on the date with your lady before the song started, you simply have to step into the picture toward the end of the song or whenever you want to ask her to dance with you. The ones who start the choreography can even be the friends who were on the date with your lady.

At the end of the song, all the dancers should have formed a circle around the two of you (even if you haven't been dancing). When the music is out, you tell your lady, that you planned this surprise together with her friends. You tell her, how you feel about her and then you get down onto your knee to ask her to marry you (all the other ladies in the circle will wish to have a boyfriend like you who plans something alike.)

After she said yes

Great, now you are already enough people to celebrate and since you are out in town anyway, you can head to the next bar. Once you have enough from the crowds, you and your beaming future wife can retreat to a quieter place.

PERSONAL NOTES

____

____

____

____

____

____

____

____

____

____

____

2. Well orchestrated

This proposal is great if your lady plays an instrument in a big band or an orchestra. Music carries emotions better than anything else anyway. Therefore, it's the perfect medium to use as a background before you ask the big question. Otherwise, it's similar to the dance flash mob.

Planning

- Get the big band or orchestra to plan a flash mob without that your lady finds out about it
- Pick a time and place where they need to show up
- Either plan a date with your lady at that time and place or get someone else to get her there.

How the proposal should play out

Your lady is at the said location, for example, the train station, with her friends at the appointed time.
All of a sudden, people from her orchestra show up and start playing a song or a medley of songs. When her first surprise is over, you step in front of her and she will be surprised all over again.
At the end of the song, the orchestra should position themselves around the two of you. Then, you tell your lady how you feel about her and why you planned this surprise. Then, it's time to get down on your knee and propose to her.

3. Hidden T-Shirts

Is your lady in a sports club? It can be anything from hockey to yoga, volleyball or gymnastics. The main thing is that it's the crew of your lady with whom she loves hanging out a few times a week. If that is the case, you have found your option for the proposal here.

Planning

- Get tight fitting shirts for the people in her sports club. On those shirts you either spell the words WILL YOU MARRY ME? (don't forget the question mark) or put complete words on the shirts (depending on how many people there are in the club).
- You plan the following scenario with the other club members without your lady finding out about it.
- Someone needs to make sure that she will attend the training that day (we all know how it is that sometimes, we suddenly aren't in the mood for sport. We don't want this to happen on the night you planned your proposal).

How the proposal should play out

On the set evening, your lady's teammates or co-sport friends will wear the tight shirt with your question below their normal sports shirt. They have to make sure that your lady doesn't see a glimpse of a shirt before it's time. At the appointed time (probably best after the warm-up), the people with the special shirts build a row in front of your lady and say that they have a surprise for her. Or rather, not them, but someone else. Then, you step into the gym. You say that you forgot to ask her something before she left for her sports lesson. You probably should have written it down, in order not to forget. Perhaps, someone here could help you with the question now. Then, the people take off their normal shirt and WILL YOU MARRY ME? Should appear in the correct order on the shirts of the sports crew.

After she said yes

There will be clapping and hugs. In that state of exhilaration which your lady now is in, it's probably not safe to do sports. So, you steal her away and go celebrate.

The others should support that decision that sport can wait until another day for this special occasion since otherwise, she might feel bad about missing an important training with her team.

4. Movie Credits

She loves watching movies so much that she even watches the credits at the end? Sometimes in the movie theater, you are the last two people in the room because everyone else has left already but she insists on watching until the screen goes black? Perhaps, then you should give her something to watch that's of more personal interest, at the end of the next movie you watch together. This proposal requires some technical knowledge. Either, you are good with video cutting yourself or you could ask a friend or even pay a designer $5 on Fiverr to do it for you.

Preparation

- Instead of telling her your words with your mouth, you will write your feelings and the proposal down in a movie editor. Then, you paste them in directly after the end of the movie (before the actual credits). You could even add some pictures or a small movie of the two of you.
- Movie theaters, unfortunately, have very strict rules about showing the movie exactly how they received it from the distributor. Therefore, your chance of them cutting your special credits in after a public viewing is very slim. But asking doesn't hurt and perhaps, at a

local, alternative movie theater you might
even get lucky.
- Have the ring ready, close by, when you are
  watching the movie. Best not in your pants
  pocket in case she fumbles around down
  there. Because then she'd find out about the
  surprise too early.
- Have some food or drinks stored away with
  which you can celebrate after she said yes.

How the proposal should play out

You sit cuddled together and watch your edited movie
(either from a stick on the TV, on the laptop or in the
movie theater.) In the end, you need to make sure
that she is focused on the screen, so perhaps, to really
grab her attention, it's a good idea if she first sees a
picture of the two of you on the screen. Afterward,
she will read the words, and, in that time, you bring
out the engagement ring (or flowers, in case you don't
do rings). When she turns her head to face you, all
excited, you get down on your knee and ask her again
whether she wants to marry you.

5. Let the pet be the messenger

Your lady has a pet with which you can cuddle? Best would be a dog or a cat but hamsters and other small animals in cages work as well.
Sometimes, the couple's dog will bring the rings to them at their wedding. We now already use the pet one step ahead of the wedding.

Planning

- You craft a ring box which you can attach to the collar of her dog or car or which you can hide in the cage of the hamster.
- Apart from the ring, you also place a note with one or two phrases telling how you feel about her, plus the question WILL YOU MARRY ME? on a small paper in the box.
- Have some champagne, wine or something special to eat ready so that you can celebrate.

How the proposal should play out

The two of you are somewhere with the cat or the dog. At some point, while the lady is busy doing something else (like going to the bathroom or taking a photo of the environment) you attach the ring box to the collar of the pet. Then, you send the pet to the lady, who hopefully notices that something is attached to the collar.

In case the pet resides in a cage, hide the ring box with the message in the hut of the animal shortly before the two of you will clean the cage. It needs to be hidden below something which she has to lift up and remove before dumping out the straw. We don't want that the ring lands in the garbage bag as well. So, when she finds the box, you act surprised. For example, "Oh, how did that get there?". You urge her to open it. You let her look at the ring and read the message. In case she doesn't get the reality of this message right away and looks at you questioningly, you now tell her some more things, why you appreciate her and want to spend the rest of your life with her, and then, you ask her again if she wants to marry you. (However, probably, she has long thrown her arms around your neck and the two of you are already in a state of bliss and the extra words are not necessary.

6. Become part of a play

Does your lady like plays or musicals? Is she even an actress herself? Then, you might want to interrupt the next show you are watching/she plays in.

Planning

In case she is in the audience:
- Contact the theater and tell them about your plan. The proposal should either happen at the beginning of the play or before the break (so that the rest of the guests can still enjoy the show as they expected it. You shouldn't need more than five minutes for the whole proposal.
- Set a date with your lady on that evening or have someone else watch the play with her and then appear on stage completely out of the blue.
- Have her sit close to the stage.
- Prepare a speech which you will say to your love.

In case she is one of the actresses:
- Contact her co-workers and let them know about your plan. That they have to keep absolutely quiet about it goes without saying.
- It would be funny if you could take the role of another actor toward the end of the play or

before the break. She will be very irritated, but the audience won't know what is going on right away.

- Remember that she has to go back to work and keep acting after she said yes. Therefore, talk with the crew about a good time for the proposal, so she can collect her feelings a little bit afterward.
- Prepare a speech which you will say to your love.

How the proposal should play out

For version number one:
If you are in the audience with her an actor will say that tonight, they need some special support from someone in the audience. He will come and get you up on stage. He might even have some fun with you to mislead the audience before you then start your speech.

In case you are hiding behind the stage while she is sitting in the audience with a friend, you wait for the cue of an actor. He could also say that he needs some special help tonight and then invite you out on stage or you could shortly take the role of someone else and for a moment only your lady will know that something strange is going on.

A spotlight should point to your lady, once you start addressing her. Propose to her from up on stage and go down to kiss her when she says yes. Or, invite her up on stage before you ask her the question up there, depending on how much attention you think she can take.

For version number two:
You previously studied the role which you will take in the play. Then, you come on stage when it's time to appear and interact with your lady. For about one minute you try to keep up the charade that you are an actual actor. Then, you stop it, apologize to the audience that you are interrupting the show, however, there is something you need to do. You quickly introduce yourself and tell your lady how you feel about her. Then, you get down on your knee and propose to her.

PERSONAL NOTES

3 UNEXPECTED SURPRISES

In this category, you find proposals which don't exactly involve a hobby, and, of course, they are romantic, but they will leave her completely speechless as she will never have expected anything like this to happen. Therefore, one of the following proposals will guarantee you the badge for "the guy who goes the extra mile". Have fun seeing the reaction of surprise in her eyes (and also of the other people who are watching, in case you pick number one or two).

1. Steal the show at a concert

Does she like listening to music or going to concerts? Is she okay with being the center of attention in a crowd of people? Then, you can make history with this proposal.

Preparation

- Contact a band of your choice two weeks to a month before the concert. This could be a band of your friends or even a big international act (who knows, maybe you get lucky and they say yes.)
- Set a date with your lady to go to this concert (or have someone else go there with her and

then, you appearing on stage will be an even bigger surprise).

- Have an awesome speech ready for when it's time to go up on stage.

How the proposal should play out

Whether you are at the concert with your lady or someone else is there with her, make sure that she is standing close to the stage.
At some point during the concert, the lead singer will invite a special guest up on stage. That is your cue. You go up on stage, quickly introduce yourself, and then invite your lady up on stage as well, since you need her, for what you planned on doing.
Probably, the people in the audience got what is about to happen and are already cheering loudly. Continue with your speech and, in the end, get down on your knee and ask her to marry you.

If your emotions had already been on a high due to the concert before, the happiness will now go over the roof and the two of you will feel as if you are walking on clouds for the rest of the evening.

2. Bake it into a cake

Which woman doesn't love cake? With this method, you could make a cupcake even sweeter and bake a cute message into it.

Preparation

- Set a date with your lady.
- Write WILL YOU MARRY ME? on a small paper slip and then wrap it into aluminum foil.
- Put together a cupcake mixture and then place the note inside the dough of one cupcake or muffin before putting them into the oven. Be sure to mark that cupcake/muffin with a toothpick or a different colored wrapper.
- You can further decorate the cupcake/muffin after it is baked, especially in case the note is visible somewhere. Make sure you always know which one the special cupcake is.

How the proposal should play out

You either cozily enjoy your cupcakes at home or you could bring them on a hike, on a paddle boat trip or wherever else you would like.
When she finds the aluminum package you urge her to unwrap it. Once she has read the words, you say your little speech which you prepared about how you feel about her. Then, you get down on your knee and propose to her.

PERSONAL NOTES

3. Melt it into ice cream

Does your lady love ice cream? Similar to the proposal with the cake, your lady will be in for another sweet surprise with this proposal. However, with the ice cream, you are a bit more tied to a place with a freezer (for example your living room).

Preparation

- Buy a tub of the favorite ice cream of your lady.
- Wrap a paper slip with WILL YOU MARRY ME? Into aluminum foil.
- Press the paper slip down into the ice cream when it's soft and then hide the path of the fork or spoon again by making the top even.
- Put the ice cream back into the freezer.
- Make sure that your lady doesn't eat the ice cream when you aren't there.

How the proposal should play out

After a nice dinner at home, during a lovely summer afternoon, or during an enjoyable movie night bring out the ice cream. Eat it together directly out of the tub with two spoons. Let her eat more and make sure that she'll be the one to spot the aluminum wrapper. When she spots it, you can act all excited and say that perhaps, it's a contest and you have won something. Urge her to unwrap it.

After she read the words you can say that you hope that she isn't disappointed that she hasn't won a contest. You tell her how you feel about her, and you propose to her.

Personal Notes

____

____

____

____

____

____

____

____

____

____

____

____

____

____

____

____

4. Hide it in the popcorn

If your lady is a laid-back person who doesn't like to draw attention to herself, and if the two of you like to sit in front of the TV and eat popcorn, you can go for this proposal.

Planning

- Have the small box with the ring hidden at home.
- Make a big bowl full of popcorn and hide the box with the ring in it (it's a bit dangerous to put the ring in there without the box, so better put the box in there, even if she will quickly find the box.)
- Have something ready to celebrate after she said yes (for example a good wine or champagne).

How the proposal should play out

As you sit in front of the TV and absentmindedly reach for the popcorn, she suddenly will feel that there is something odd in the bowl. Quickly, she will realize what this small box means. After she opens it and spots the ring, you tell her how you feel about her, then you get down on your knee and ask her if she will marry you.

5. Let her solve the riddle

Does she like mysteries? Is she enthusiastic about scavenger hunts, geocaching or escape rooms? In that case, you can plan a very personal quest for her.

Preparation

- Plan a scavenger hunt with several clues she needs to find and riddles she has to solve until she reaches a location where you are hiding. You can plan this scavenger hunt with a friend in case you don't like to be creative yourself.
- Get some friends together who will go on the quest with your lady while you, unfortunately, are prevented from coming because you are out of town because of your job, a friend's birthday, etc. It would even be a bigger surprise if she thinks you are out of the country for the weekend.
- The friends can pretend that they found the quest on the internet and want to try it or that it's something they plan for another friend's birthday and have to try out before she can do it.
- If you don't want to go through all this trouble yourself, you can also book an escape room with several rooms. Your lady will go to the escape room with friends (again thinking that you are out of the country) and you will be waiting in the last room. The friends and the person in charge of the room just have to make sure that the group makes it to the last room.

How the proposal should play out

While the group of friends is on the quest, a group
member can keep you updated about the progress via
messages on the phone. The group should make sure
that the lady is the one who solves the last riddle and
then finds your hiding place. She will be very surprised
to see you since you aren't even supposed to be in the
country. You tell her your feelings and then get down
on your knee and propose to her.

PERSONAL NOTES

____

____

____

____

____

____

____

____

____

____

____

____

6. Surprise via the speakers (train or plane)

Does your lady sometimes travel on the train or plane? If she isn't bothered by getting some public attention you can surprise her with this proposal.

Planning

- Find out exactly which train or plane she will take on a certain day.
- Contact the train service or the airline and ask them whether you can propose to your girlfriend over the speakers. On the plane, it will be a lot more difficult due to safety regulations. They might ask you to buy a ticket and fly as well and since you don't want her to see you in the waiting or boarding area, you have to figure something out with the crew. Yet, it's not impossible.
- If you want to do the proposal on the train, have a friend keep an eye on her, so that you know in which wagon she sits.
- Prepare a speech which you will say through the speakers.

How the proposal should play out

On the train:
The friend who keeps an eye on your lady or is accompanying her on the trip will keep you up to date via the phone about where they are.

When the train is rolling, you will start your speech by asking for the attention of FIRST and LAST name of your lady. The friend can help to make her listen in case she had her headphones on and didn't register the announcement. Then, you tell her your feelings. It would be best if you were standing at the end of the same wagon or one very close to her. At the end of the speech, you say that you will ask her the main purpose of this speech in person now. You go find her and when you are in front of her, you go down on your knee and ask her to marry you.

On the plane:

Here, it's probably best to do the proposal while you're still docked to the departure port, once everyone is on board. You can call her name via the speaker of the flight attendants while not showing yourself to her. You say that there is something wrong with her seat as she is sitting next to the wrong person. By now, she might have recognized your voice, but she will be too confused about what is going on. Therefore, you step somewhere where she can see you (in case it's behind her, you have to tell her to turn around). Afterward, you tell her your feelings and you ask her to marry you.

The best thing then would be, if the airline gave the two of you a free upgrade and you could spend the flight celebrating in the business class. Or perhaps, you aren't even flying with her and have to leave the plane again (however, it's quite harsh to be separated after such a development, and therefore, you should definitely buy a ticket in the first place and fly with her.

PERSONAL NOTES

____

____

____

____

____

____

____

____

____

____

____

____

Afterthoughts

Now that you have read all those suggestions for a proposal, I hope you feel ready to take the next step in your life. You no doubt will be nervous when it's time to pronounce this four-word question. But therefore, you have clear preparation guidelines for each proposal and won't forget anything. The only other thing I can recommend you is to talk to your friends about your plan. It's an exciting step. Share it with them to receive their moral support and also so that you can function as a role model for them. Perhaps, then they'll also think of planning a surprise for their girlfriend.

Secondly, you could watch some YouTube marriage proposal videos to see what kind of deep emotions you will create with your proposal. Not many men can claim that they have truly moved other people during their life. Also, you will see that there are some wedding proposals online where the girl said no. If you received this book from your lady or one of your lady's friends, you can be sure that it's her deepest wish to marry you. However, in case the proposal was your idea all along, I hope you have lately asked your lady, what her answer would be in case you would ask her to marry you and how she pictures her future with you. Getting married is a big step, and of course, I am strongly rooting for special marriage proposals and spending a faithful, happy and supportive life together, but your lady might not think like me.

Therefore, just ask her about her plans in a simple conversation, before you start contacting any big pop bands about interrupting their show. And then, if you know her answer will be yes, have fun planning this surprise. Know that she will love it and therefore, you should enjoy every second of this whole process.
From secretly planning it, to seeing the surprise in her face, and then getting her very happy yes as an answer.

Do you need more info?

In case you need more info, I am happy to help as far as I can. Contact or follow me through these channels:

(b) www.swissmissontour.com
(i) @swissmissontour
(f) SwissMissOnTour
(w) www.slgigerbooks.wordpress.com

Was this guide helpful?

In case you liked this guidebook, I'd greatly appreciate a positive review on Amazon. Thank you very much! 😊

More books by S. L. Giger

Receive a free packing list

Never forget anything important ever again and don't waste unnecessary time with packing. Send an e-mailt with the subject: packing list and receive a free packing list along with a sample of my Thailand travel guide.

Send the e-mail to swissmissstories@gmail.com and receive your free gift.